Folk Songs

Exclusive Distributors:
Music Sales Limited
8/9 Frith Street, London W1V 5TZ, England.
Music Sales Corporation
225 Park Avenue South,
New York, NY 10003, United States of America.
Music Sales Pty Limited
120 Rothschild Avenue, Rosebery, NSW 2018, Australia.

This book © Copyright 1993 by
Wise Publications
Order No. AM91366
ISBN 0-7119-3629-3

Book design by Hutton Staniford
Compiled by Peter Evans
Music arranged by Stephen Duro
Music processed by Interactive Sciences Limited, Gloucester

Cover photograph by Mick Booth

Music Sales' complete catalogue lists thousands of titles and is free from your local music shop,
or direct from Music Sales Limited. Please send a cheque/postal order for £1.50 for postage to:
Music Sales Limited, Newmarket Road, Bury St. Edmunds, Suffolk IP33 3YB.

Your Guarantee of Quality:
As publishers, we strive to produce every book to the highest commercial standards.

The music has been freshly engraved and the book has been carefully designed to minimise
awkward page turns and to make playing from it a real pleasure.

Particular care has been given to specifying acid-free, neutral-sized paper made from pulps which have not been elemental
chlorine bleached. This pulp is from farmed sustainable forests and was produced with special regard for the environment.
Throughout, the printing and binding have been planned to ensure a sturdy, attractive publication which should give years of
enjoyment.

If your copy fails to meet our high standards, please inform us and we will gladly replace it.

Printed in the United Kingdom by
Halstan & Co Limited, Amersham, Buckinghamshire.

Annie Laurie

Traditional

With expression

The Max - well - ton braes are bon - nie, where ear - ly fa's the dew, And it's there that An - nie Lau - rie Gi'ed me her pro - mise true, Gi'ed

2. Her brow is like the snow-drift
   Her neck is like the swan,
   Her face it is the fairest
   That e'er the sun shone on,
   That e'er the sun shone on,
   And dark blue is her e'e,
   And for bonnie Annie Laurie
   I'd lay me down and dee.

3. Like dew on the gowan lying,
   Is the fa' o' her fairy feet;
   And like winds in summer sighing,
   Her voice is low and sweet,
   Her voice is low and sweet,
   An' she's a' the world to me;
   And for bonnie Annie Laurie
   I'd lay me down and dee.

The Ash Grove

Traditional

Moderately

As I Walked Through The Meadows

Traditional

Moderately

1. As I walked thru' the mea-dows to take the fresh air, The flow-ers were bloom-ing and gay;— I heard a young dam-sel so sweet-ly a-sing-ing, Her cheeks like the blos-som in May.— I

2. So she tripped along with her dear little feet,
   But I followed and soon I drew near;
   I called her so pretty, my true love so sweet,
   That she took me at last for her dear.
   I took the fair maid by the lily-white hand,
   On the green mossy bank we sat down,
   I gave her a kiss on her sweet rosy lips:
   A tree spread its branches around.

3. Now when we did rise from that green bushy grove,
   In the meadows we wandered away,
   And I placed my true love on a primèrose bank,
   While I picked her a handful of may.
   The very next morning I made her my bride,
   Just after the breaking of day;
   The bells they did ring and the birds they did sing
   As I crowned her the Queen of sweet May.

The Bluebells Of Scotland

Traditional

2. Oh where, tell me where, did your Highland laddie dwell?
   Oh where, tell me where, did your Highland laddie dwell?
   He dwelt in bonnie Scotland, where blooms the sweet bluebell,
   And it's oh in my heart I lo'e my laddie well.
   (*repeat last two lines*)

3. Oh what, tell me what, does your Highland laddie wear?
   Oh what, tell me what, does your Highland laddie wear?
   A bonnet with a lofty plume, and on his breast a plaid,
   And it's oh in my heart I lo'e my Highland lad.
   (*repeat last two lines*)

4. Oh what, tell me what, if your Highland lad be slain?
   Oh what, tell me what, if your Highland lad be slain?
   Oh, no! true love will be his guard and bring him safe again,
   For it's oh my heart would break if my Highland lad were slain.
   (*repeat last two lines*)

My Bonnie, Bonnie Boy

Traditional

2. 'Twas up the green valley and down the green grove
   Like one that was troubled in mind,
   She whooped and she halloed and she played upon her pipe,
   But no bonnie boy could she find,
   But no bonnie boy could she find.

3. She looked up high, and she looked down low,
   The sun did shine wonderful warm,
   Whom should she spy there but her bonnie, bonnie boy,
   So close in another girl's arm,
   So close in another girl's arm.

4. My bonnie, bonnie boy is gone over the sea,
   I fear I shan't see him again;
   But were I to have him, or were I to not,
   I will think of him once now and then,
   I will think of him once now and then.

Cockles And Mussels

Traditional

Not too slow

2. She was a fishmonger,
   But sure t'was no wonder,
   For so were her father and mother before,
   And they each wheel'd their barrow
   Thro' streets broad and narrow
   Crying cockles and mussels! Alive, alive, O!

3. She died of a fever,
   And no one could save her,
   And that was the end of sweet Molly Malone,
   But her ghost wheels her barrow
   Thro' streets broad and narrow,
   Crying cockles and mussels! Alive, alive, O!

Cold Blows The Wind

Traditional

Moderately

1. Cold

blows the wind o'er my true— love, Cold— blow the drops of— rain;—— I

ne - ver, ne - ver had but one true— love, And in Cam - vile— he was— slain.—— I'd

do as much for my true— love as— an - y young girl may;—— I'll

2. But when twelve months were come and gone,
   This young man he arose,
   'What makes you weep down by my grave?
   I can't take my repose.'
   'One kiss, one kiss of your lily-white lips,
   One kiss is all I crave;
   One kiss, one kiss of your lily-white lips,
   And return back to your grave.'

3. 'My lips they are as cold as clay,
   My breath is heavy and strong;
   If thou wast to kiss my lily-white lips,
   The days would not be long!'
   'O don't you remember the garden grove,
   Where we was used to walk?
   Pluck the finest flower of them all,
   'Twill wither to a stalk.'

4. 'Go fetch me a nut from a dungeon keep,
   And water from a stone,
   And white milk from a maiden's breast
   That babe bare never none.'
   'Go dig me a grave both wide and deep,
   (As quickly as you may)
   I will lie down in it and take one sleep
   For a twelve month and a day.'

The Cuckoo

Traditional

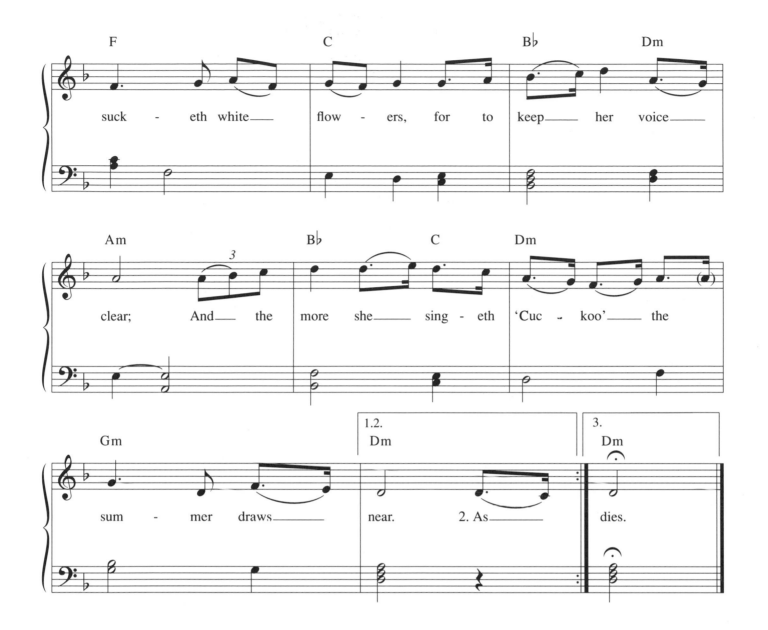

2. As I was a-walking and a-talking one day,
   I met my own true love, as he came that way.
   O to meet him was a pleasure, though the courting was a woe,
   For I found him false hearted, he would kiss me and go.

3. I wish I were a scholar and could handle the pen,
   I would write to my lover and to all roving men.
   I would tell them of the grief and woe that attend on their lies,
   I would wish them have pity on the flower when it dies.

The Derby Ram

Traditional

Jolly

f

1. As

I was going to Der - by, Sir, 'twas on a sum - mer's day. I met the fin - est ram, Sir, that ev - er was fed on hay; And in - deed, Sir, 'tis true, Sir, I

Chorus

2. It had four feet to walk on, Sir, it had four feet to stand,
   And every foot it had, Sir, did cover an acre of land.
   (*Chorus*)

3. The horns that were on its head, Sir, held a regiment of men,
   And the tongue that was in its head, Sir, would feed them every one.
   (*Chorus*)

4. The wool that was on its back, Sir, made fifty packs of cloth,
   And for to tell a lie, Sir, I'm sure I'm very loth.
   (*Chorus*)

5. The wool that was on its sides, Sir, made fifty more complete,
   And it was sent to Russia to clothe the Emperor's fleet.
   (*Chorus*)

6. The tail was fifty yards, Sir, as near as I can tell,
   And it was sent to Rome, Sir, to ring Saint Peter's bell.
   (*Chorus*)

Early One Morning

Traditional

Moderately

treat— a poor— mai - den so?'   2. Re - mem - ber the
4. Thus sang the poor

vows— that you made— to your Ma - ry, Re - mem - ber the
mai - den, her sor - row be - wail - ing, Thus sang the poor

bow'r— where you vowed— to be true.   'Oh! don't de -
maid— in the val - ley be - low.

ceive— me! Oh! nev - er leave— me! How— could you

treat— a— poor— mai - den so?'   3. Oh, poor— mai - den so?'

Feast Song

Traditional

Moderately

mf

1. Our— sheep - shear-ing done, to our mas - ter we come, who en -
joins us to sport as we please;——— Then be - side plough and flail o'er our
fleece and our pail We will boast of our fine wool and cheese.——— Our sweet

Chorus

2. Should your wishes incline to beer, cider, or wine,
   As you sit with your pipe at your ease,
   Their true flavour to find always keep this in mind,
   Clear your taste with a bit of old cheese.
   (*Chorus*)

3. Join hands then, unite with joy and delight,
   This happy occasion we'll seize,
   And with am'rous desire we will drink
   'May our Squire live long, and enjoy his own cheese!'
   (*Chorus*)

The Green Bushes

Traditional

Moderately

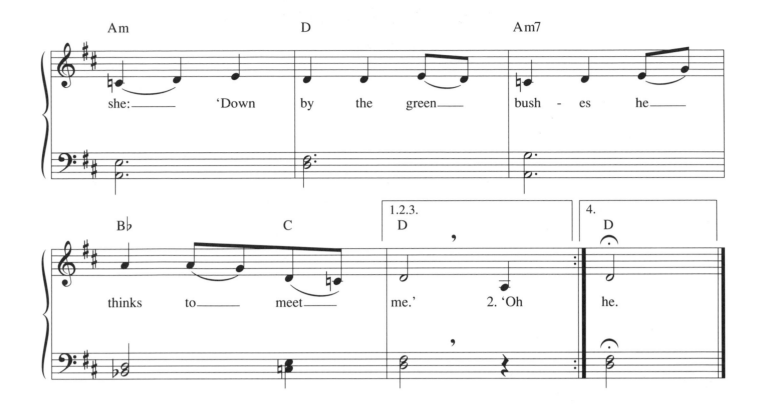

2. 'Oh, where are you going, my pretty maid?'
   'My lover I'm seeking, kind Sir,' she said.
   'Shall I be your lover, and will you agree
   To forsake the old love, and foregather with me?'

3. 'Quick, let us be moving from under the trees,
   Quick let us be moving kind Sir, if you please;
   For yonder my true love is coming, I see,
   Down by the green bushes he thinks to meet me.'

4. The old love arrived, the maiden was gone,
   He sighed very deeply, he sighed all alone,
   'She is on with another, before off with me,
   So adieu ye green bushes, for ever,' said he.

Greensleeves

Traditional

2. I have been ready at your hand
   To grant whatever you would crave,
   I have both wagèd life and land,
   Your love and goodwill for to have.
   (*Chorus*)

3. I bought thee kerchers to thy head
   That were wrought fine and gallantly;
   I kept thee booth at board and bed,
   Which cost my purse well favour'dly.
   (*Chorus*)

4. Well, I will pray to God on high,
   That thou my constancy may'st see,
   And that yet once before I die
   Thou wilt vouchsafe to love me.
   (*Chorus*)

Ground For The Floor

Traditional

2. My cot is surrounded with bramble and thorn,
   And sweet are the notes of the birds in the morn;
   I've a guinea in my pocket and plenty more in store,
   If you look down below you'll find ground for the floor.

3. My bed's made of straw my limbs to repose
   And as for myself I've but one suit of clothes;
   And that's made of ticking, all stitched up secure,
   If you look down below you'll find ground for the floor.

Harvest Song

Traditional

With movement

The Lark In The Morn

Traditional

With movement

I____ was a - walk - ing one morn - ing in the spring, I

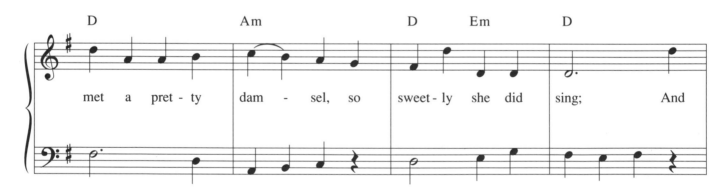

met a pret - ty dam - sel, so sweet - ly she did sing; And

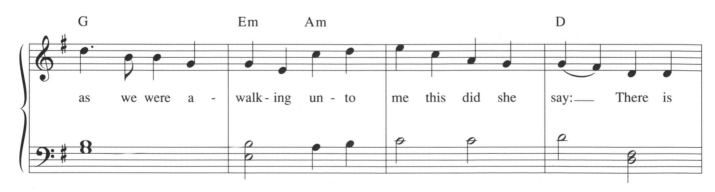

as we were a - walk - ing un - to me this did she say:____ There is

no life like the plough-boy's all in the month of May. The
lark___ in the morn___ she will rise up from her nest, And
mount up on the air___ with the dew all on her breast; And
like the pret-ty plough-boy she will whis-tle and will sing,___ And at
night she will re-turn___ to her own nest back a-gain.

The Lincolnshire Poacher

Traditional

Jolly

1. When I was bound apprentice in famous Lincolnshire, I served my master truly for nearly seven long year, Till

2. As me and my companions were setting of a snare,
   The game-keeper was watching us, for him we did not care;
   For we can wrestle and fight, my boys, and jump out anywhere;
   For it's my delight of a shiny night in the season of the year.

3. Well, here's success to poaching, for I do think it fair;
   Bad luck to ev'ry game-keeper that would not sell his deer;
   Good luck to ev'ry housekeeper that wants to buy a hare;
   And it's my delight of a shiny night in the season of the year.

I'll Tell You Of A Fellow

Traditional

2. Last night he came to see me, he made so long a stay,
   That I really thought the blockhead would never go away;
   He said it would be jolly as we journey up the hill
   To go hand in hand together, but I hardly think it will.

3. He talkèd of devotion, devotion pure and deep,
   To me it seemed so silly, I nearly fell asleep;
   The tears the creature wasted was enough to turn a mill,
   Yet he urges me to have him, but I hardly think I will.

4. He told me of a cottage, of a cottage in the trees,
   And don't you think this fellow fell down upon his knees?
   He said we should be happy as we journey up the hill
   To be always with each other, but I hardly think I will.

5. You know I would not choose him, but that I'm fairly in it,
   For he says if I refuse him he could not live a minute;
   And there are the commandments which say you must not kill,
   So I've thought the matter over and I really think I will.

O No John!

Traditional

With movement

3. O madam , I will give you jewels;
   I will make you rich and free;
   I will give you silken dresses,
   Madam, will you marry me?
       O No John! No John! No John! No!

4. O madam since you are so cruel,
   And that you do scorn me so,
   If I may not be your lover,
   Madam, will you let me go?
       O No John! No John! No John! No!

5. Then I will stay with you for ever,
   If you will not be unkind.
   Madam, I have vowed to love you;
   Would you have me change my mind?
       O No John! No John! No John! No!

6. O hark! I hear the church bells ringing;
   Will you come and be my wife?
   Or, dear madam, have you settled
   To live single all your life?
       O No John! No John! No John! No!

The Skye Boat Song

Traditional

2. Though the waves leap, soft shall ye sleep,
   Ocean's a royal bed;
   Rocked in the deep, Flora will keep
   Watch by your weary head.
   (*Chorus*)

3. Many's the lad fought on that day,
   Well the claymore could wield
   When the night came, silently lay
   Dead on Culloden's field.
   (*Chorus*)

4. Burned are our homes, exile and death
   Scatter the loyal men;
   Yet, e'er the sword cool in the sheath,
   Charlie will come again.
   (*Chorus*)

Twankydillo

Traditional

Jolly

health to the jol- ly black- smith, the best of all fel- lows, who works at his

an - vil while the boy blows the bel- lows; Which makes my bright

ham- mer to rise and to fall, Here's to old Cole, and to young Cole, and to

2. If a gentleman calls his horse for to shoe,
   He makes no denial of one pot or two,
   For it makes my bright hammer to rise and to fall,
   Here's to old Cole, and to young Cole, and to old Cole of all,
   Twankydillo, twankydillo, twankydillo, dillo, dillo, dillo.
   And he that loves strong beer is a hearty good fellow.

3. Here's a health to King Charlie and likewise his queen,
   And to all the royal little ones where'er they are seen;
   Which makes my bright hammer to rise and to fall
   Here's to old Cole, and to young Cole, and to old Cole of all,
   Twankydillo, twankydillo, twankydillo, dillo, dillo, dillo.
   A roaring pair of bagpipes made of green willow.

The Wassail Bough

Traditional

2. I have a little purse, it is made of leather skin;
   I want a little sixpence, to line it well within.
   (*Chorus*)

3. Bring us out the table, and spread it with the cloth;
   Bring us out the bread and cheese, and a bit of your Christmas loaf.
   (*Chorus*)

4. God bless the master of the house, and the mistress too;
   Also the little children, which round the table grew.
   (*Chorus*)